WONDER
STARTERS

Butterflies

Pictures by **JOHN MOUSDALE**

Published by **WONDER BOOKS**
A Division of Grosset & Dunlap, Inc.

51 Madison Avenue   New York, N.Y. 10010

Published in the United States by Wonder Books, a Division
of Grosset & Dunlap, Inc.

ISBN: 0-448-09673-0 (Trade Edition)
ISBN: 0-448-06393-X (Library Edition)

FIRST PRINTING 1973

Printed and bound in the United States.

Library of Congress Catalog Card Number: 73-1980

I can see a butterfly.
It is on a flower.

1

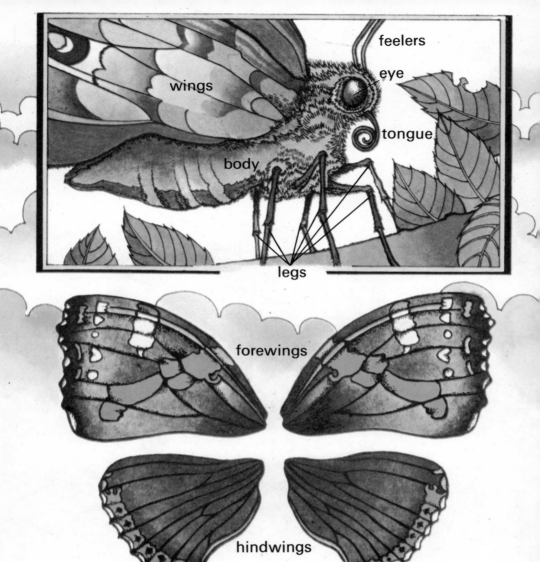

feelers

eye

wings

tongue

body

legs

forewings

hindwings

Butterflies have six legs.
They have four wings.
The wings often have beautiful colors.
2

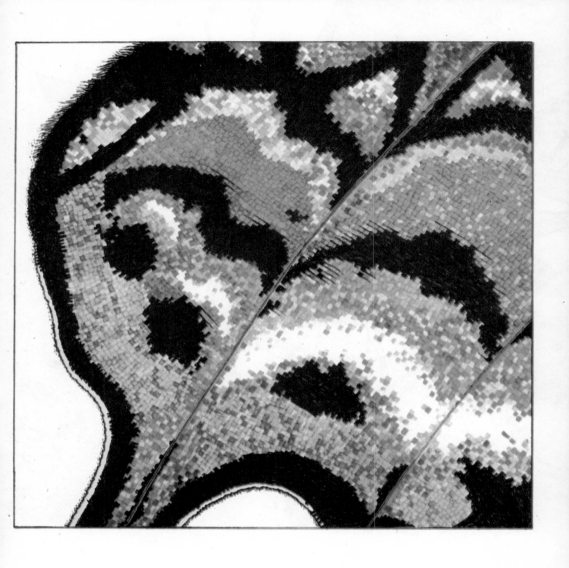

Butterflies' wings
have tiny scales all over them.

3

Most butterflies
drink nectar from flowers.
They have long tongues for drinking.
4

Female butterflies lay eggs.
They often lay them on leaves.

When the eggs hatch
caterpillars come out.
At first the caterpillars
are very small.
6

Most caterpillars eat leaves.
The caterpillars grow big.

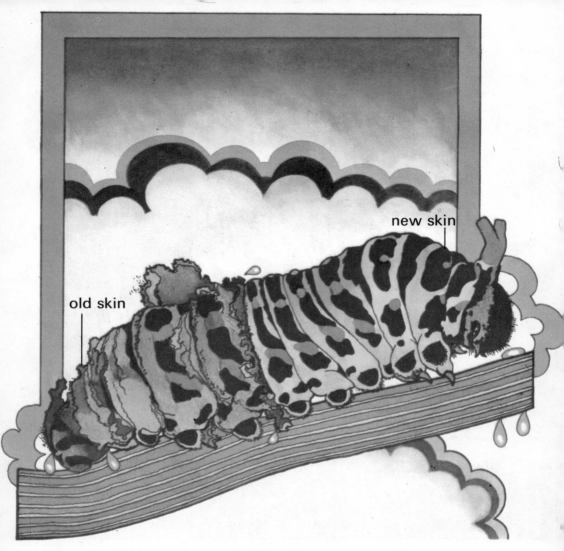

old skin

new skin

When the caterpillars grow big
they need a bigger skin.
The old skin comes off.
There is a new skin underneath.
8

The caterpillar forms
a hard outer case for itself.
Inside the case, the caterpillar
turns into a butterfly.

The butterfly comes out.
It spreads its wings
and flies away.

10

Orange tip

Mountain ringlet

Skipper

Swallowtail

Tortoiseshell

Blue

There are many kinds
of butterflies.
Here are some of them.

This butterfly
lives in a hot country.
It is very big.
It is called a Birdwing.

This white butterfly
is quite small.
It lays eggs on cabbages.
The caterpillars eat the cabbages.

13

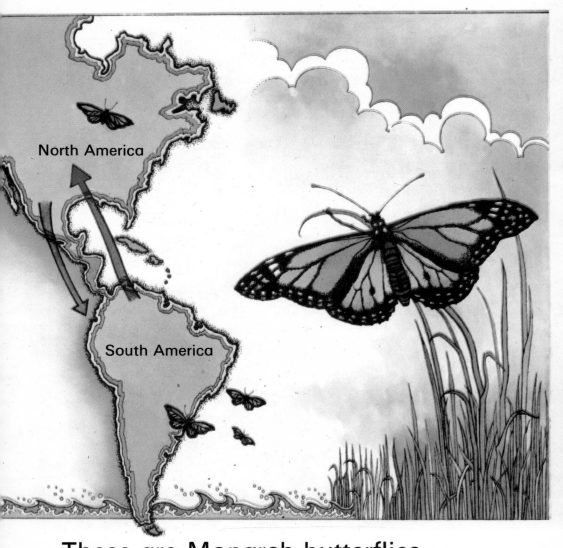

These are Monarch butterflies.
They live in America.
They fly south in autumn.
They fly north in spring.

14

This is a peacock butterfly.
It has patterns on its wings.
The patterns look like
the patterns on a peacock's tail.

Here are some moths.
Moths are like butterflies.
But their wings are different.
16

These caterpillars
will be moths one day.
They have made a big web
like a spider's web.

These moth caterpillars
live on trees in a wood.
There are too many caterpillars.
They have eaten nearly all the leaves.
18

These are clothes moths.
They lay eggs on clothes.
The eggs hatch.
The caterpillars eat the clothes.

Many moths fly about at night.
They often fly into lights.
20

Some moths fly about
in the day.
They often have beautiful colors.

21

See for yourself.
Find a caterpillar.
Feed it on the kind of leaves
you found it on.
Watch it grow up.
22

Starter's **Butterflies** words

butterfly
(page 1)

flower
(page 1)

legs
(page 2)

eyes
(page 2)

feelers
(page 2)

tongue
(page 2)

body
(page 2)

wings
(page 2)

scales
(page 3)

drink
(page 4)

nectar
(page 4)

eggs
(page 5)

leaf
(page 5)

caterpillar
(page 6)

eat
(page 7)

skin
(page 8)

case
(page 9)

fly
(page 10)

Swallowtail
(page 11)

Birdwing
(page 12)

Monarch
butterfly
(page 14)

spider
(page 17)

Peacock
butterfly
(page 15)

tree
(page 18)

peacock
(page 15)

wood
(page 18)

moth
(page 16)

clothes
(page 19)

web
(page 17)

light
(page 20)